Have fun with Arts and Crafts

Arts and Crafts

BIRMINGHAM DISCARDED BOOK SH LIBRARY SERVICES

Knights and Castles

Rita Storey

W
FRANKLIN WATTS
LONDON·SYDNEY

C2 000 004 831050

This edition 2013

First published in 2012 by
Franklin Watts
338 Euston Road
London NW1 3BH

Franklin Watts Australia
Level 17/207 Kent Street
Sydney NSW 2000

Copyright © Franklin Watts 2012
All rights reserved.
Series editor: Amy Stephenson

Packaged for Franklin Watts by Storeybooks
rita@storeybooks.co.uk
Designer: Rita Storey
Editor: Nicola Barber
Crafts: Rita Storey
Photography: Tudor Photography, Banbury
www.tudorphotography.co.uk

A CIP catalogue record for this book is available
from the British Library.

Printed in China

Dewey classification:745.5
ISBN 978 1 4451 2697 5

Cover images: Shutterstock (top left), Tudor Photography, Banbury

Franklin Watts is a division of Hachette Children's Books,
an Hachette UK company
www.hachette.co.uk

Before you start

Some of the projects in this book require scissors, paint, glue
and a sewing needle. When using these things we would
recommend that children are supervised by a responsible
adult. Where a project requires the use of a craft knife
(pp4 – 5, 8 – 9 and 12 – 13) this must be used by
a responsible adult.

Contents

Medieval Castle 4

Coat of Arms 6

Defend Yourself 8

A Knight's Helmet 10

A Fine Sword 12

Ready for Battle 14

Knight's Castle Card 16

Crazy Catapult 18

Jester's Hat Prints 20

Roary the Dragon 22

Jousting 24

Drawstring Purses 26

Castle Picture 28

Templates 30

Further Information & Index 32

Medieval Castle

In the Middle Ages knights lived in castles with thick stone walls and tall towers. You can make your own fantastic castle complete with battlements, towers and a gatehouse to keep out the fiercest army.

For a castle stronghold you will need

- a craft knife (ask an adult to use the knife)
- large cardboard box
- 4 large cardboard crisp tubes
- ruler
- paint
- paintbrush
- small cardboard box
- 2 cardboard tubes from inside a kitchen roll
- thin silver card
- double-sided tape
- sticky tape
- glue
- scissors
- coloured paper and cocktail sticks to make the flags

1 Using the scissors or the craft knife cut the top off the large cardboard box so that the sides are 4cm shorter than the cardboard crisp tubes. Cut down each corner of the box to make four flaps as shown.

Cardboard can be hard to cut, so ask a grown-up to help you with this.

2 Cut a strip 2cm wide off both sides of each flap. Paint both sides of the flaps of the opened-out cardboard box. Leave to dry.

3 Paint the four crisp tubes, the small box and the two smaller tubes. Leave to dry.

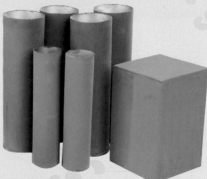

4 To make the tops of the towers, or battlements, cut four strips of silver card long enough to wrap around a crisp tube. The strips should be 3cm deep. Cut rectangles out of the top edge of each strip, equally spaced to look like the ones in this picture. Use double-sided tape to attach a strip to the top of each tube.

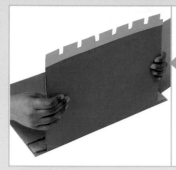

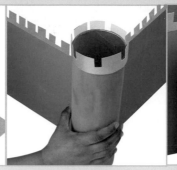

5 Cut four more strips of silver card the same length as the four sides of the large cardboard box. Each strip should be 3cm deep. Then follow the instructions in step 4 to cut out the battlements. Glue a strip to the top of each side of the large box.

6 Cut two strips of card long enough to wrap around a small tube. Each strip should be 1.5cm deep. Cut small rectangles out of the top edge of each strip (see step 4). Using double-sided tape attach a strip to the top of each of the small tubes.

7 Using sticky tape attach the four crisp tubes to the four corners of the box. Make sure the tape is on the inside of the box so that it does not show.

8 Glue the small cardboard box to the middle of the front of your castle. This will be your gatehouse. Glue a small cardboard tube on either side of the small box.

Get ready to protect your castle against the enemy!

9 Paint narrow windows on the towers. Cut strips of silver card and glue them together to make a portcullis. Shape the top to look like the one in the picture opposite. Glue it on to the gatehouse.

10 Use the template on page 31 to cut out flags from folded coloured paper. Make sure the short, straight edge of the template is on the fold on your paper. Spread them with glue and fold them over a cocktail stick. Attach them to the inside of the towers with sticky tape.

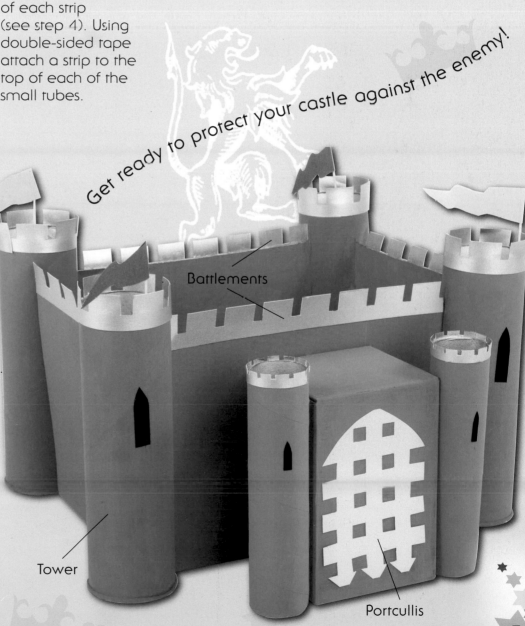

Battlements

Tower

Portcullis

Coat of Arms

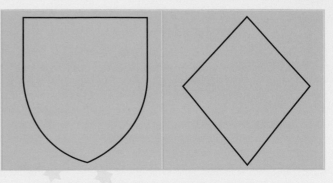

A coat of arms is a design made up of shapes and symbols. A knight had his own coat of arms on his shield and tunic. His followers wore his coat of arms, too. In battle, a coat of arms was useful for showing who was fighting on each side – it was hard to recognise people wearing helmets and armour! Create your own coat of arms to hang on your bedroom door.

For a coat of arms design you will need

- large sheets of paper
- scissors
- ruler
- glue
- felt-tip pens, pencils or crayons
- paints and paintbrushes
- gold or silver paint
- coloured paper

1 Choose a shape for your coat of arms and draw it on the large sheet of paper. Cut it out.

2 Either paint or colour the whole shape or divide it into sections, like the ones shown above. Then paint or colour the sections in two contrasting colours.

3 Paint a cross, a thick stripe or a chevron with either gold or silver paint on a large piece of paper. Leave to dry. Using your coat of arms shape as a guide, cut out the stripe or chevron so that it will fit your shape. Glue it to your coat of arms shape.

4 Think of some pictures that tell other people about your hobbies and interests. Draw a symbol for each one on the coloured paper and cut out the shapes.

5 Glue the symbols on to the gold or silver part of your design.

6 Copy the helmet design from the template on page 32 (or download a colour version at www.franklinwatts.co.uk). Put it around your coat of arms to show that you are a knight.

Coat of Arms Design

The design of every coat of arms is unique to its owner. By looking at a coat of arms, an expert can find out a lot about who owns it. Today, schools, universities and other organisations often have coats of arms. Your school may have one.

Defend Yourself

When a knight went into battle he carried a strong shield for protection from swords and arrows. Make this brilliant shield and get ready to defend yourself.

To make this sturdy shield you will need

- large sheet of paper
- pencil
- scissors
- big piece of poster board
- craft knife (ask an adult to use it)
- ruler
- glue
- 4 sheets of coloured paper, 2 in each colour
- silver duct tape
- strong card

1 Fold the paper in half. Starting at the fold, draw the shape of half a shield on the paper. Cut along the line you have drawn and open out the shape.

2 Draw round the shape on to the board. Ask an adult to cut out the shape using a sharp craft knife.

 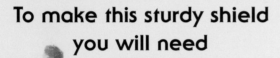

3 Using a ruler, divide the shield into four quarters.

4 Cover the front of the shield with glue and stick a piece of paper on to each quarter of the shield. Use the lines you have drawn to line up your paper.

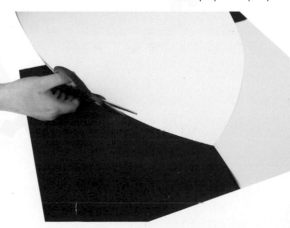

5 Turn the shape over and carefully trim off the excess paper.

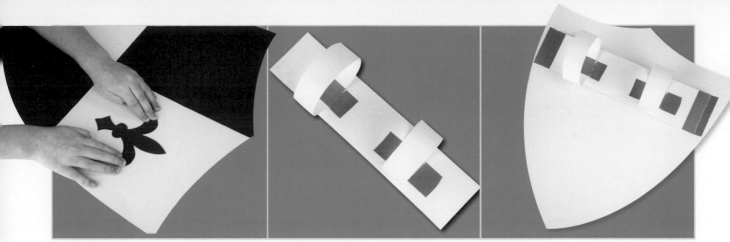

6 Use silver duct tape to make a cross in the centre of the shield. The cross should stretch from top to bottom and from left to right. Copy four shapes from page 30 on to the leftover pieces of coloured paper. Cut them out. Glue one on each quarter of the shield. If you prefer, you can use your own coat of arms design (see pages 6 – 7).

7 Cut a piece of card 4cm shorter than the width of the top of the shield and 10cm deep. Cut two strips of card, each one long enough to go round your arm with a little room to spare. Tape them into circles. Attach the circles to the piece of card with duct tape so that you can slide your arm through one and hold on to the other.

8 Tape this cardboard panel as close as possible to each edge on the back of the shield. Because the panel is shorter than the width of the shield it will make the shield curve a bit.

Have your shield ready to stop any swords that may come your way.

From Page to Squire

Boys chosen to train as knights usually left home at the age of seven. They became pages (assistants) to grand knights and lived in their castles. Pages had a lot to learn. They were taught good manners, and how to read and write. At the age of fourteen pages became squires. This was when they began to learn the skills of fighting and jousting.

A Knight's Helmet

This fearsome helmet will frighten your enemies and protect your head at the same time. Knights wore helmets to fend off cuts from swords and knives.

To make a knight's helmet you will need

- compass
- felt-tip pen
- silver card
- scissors
- ruler
- sticky tape
- gold paper
- glue

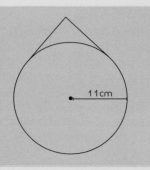

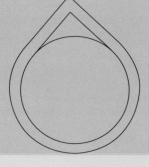

1 To make the headpiece open the compass out to 11cm and draw a circle on to the back of the silver card. Draw a triangle out of the top of your circle to make a teardrop shape.

2 Draw a line 1cm outside the edge of the teardrop shape and cut out along this line.

3 Cut triangular slits from the outside to the inner line to make tabs all around the shape.

4 Using a ruler, draw two lines from the middle of the circle (where the compass point was) to the outside of the circle, about 4cm apart and directly opposite the point on the shape. Cut out the triangle of card between these two lines.

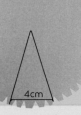

5 Bend the tabs down along the original outline.

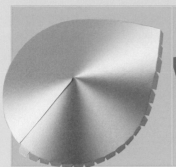

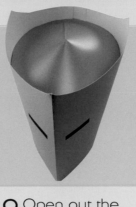

6 Bring the straight edges together and fasten at the back with sticky tape to make a cone shape.

7 To make the main part of the helmet, cut a rectangle of silver card about 25cm by 70cm. Fold it in half so that the short edges meet each other. Shape the top edge as shown above. Decide where you want your eye slits to be. Cut out the two slits.

8 Open out the card. Fit the fold to the point at the front of the headpiece. Tape the tabs on to the inside of the main part of the helmet. Tape the back of the helmet together.

9 Copy the shape on page 30 on to gold paper. Make three of these shapes and stick them on to the points of the helmet. Cut out two thick cross shapes from gold paper. Snip off the corners and glue the shapes on to the sides of the helmet.

Your scary helmet will frighten off enemies.

To become a fully-fledged knight, make the sword on pages 12 – 13 to go with your shield and helmet.

From Squire to Knight

When a squire became a knight he was given the title 'Sir' in front of his name. Today, some countries still reward bravery or loyal service by making people knights. In the United Kingdom special 'knighting' ceremonies are held at New Year and on the Queen's official birthday. The person to be knighted kneels before the Queen, who touches both their shoulders with a ceremonial sword.

A Fine Sword

On the battlefield knights often carried big swords called broadswords. This type of sword was so heavy that a knight had to hold it with both hands to swing it round and fight with it. A broadsword had sharp edges and a pointed tip. This sword looks the same – but it is a lot less dangerous!

To make this fine fighting sword you will need

- side of a cardboard box 15cm x 50cm
- felt-tip pen
- scissors or craft knife (ask an adult to use it)
- thick card
- glue
- roll of wide duct tape
- ribbon
- stick-on jewels

1 Draw the blade of a sword on the cardboard. Cut it out. Use this cutout as a template to draw round and make a second, identical shape.

2 Draw the handle of a sword on a piece of card. It should be about a quarter of the length of your sword blade. Cut it out. Use this cutout as a template to draw round and make a second identical shape.

3 Spread glue on one of the blade shapes and stick the other one on top of it.

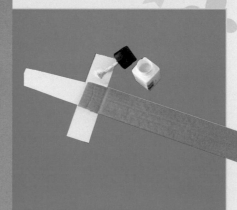

4 Glue one of the handle pieces to the top of the blade. Then spread glue all over the rest of the handle and glue the second piece on top, sandwiching the blade in the middle.

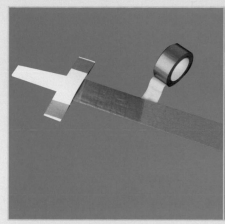

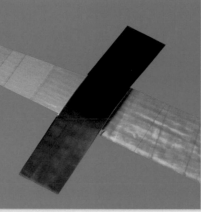

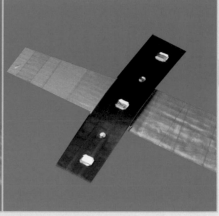

5 Tape the edges of the handle together to make sure they are secured. Tightly wrap the whole sword in silver duct tape.

6 Spread glue on both sides of the guard. Wrap ribbon around the guard. Leave to dry.

7 Decorate the guard with stick-on jewels.

Grip

Guard

Use this sword wisely like a brave knight.

Blade

The Tales of King Arthur

No-one knows who King Arthur really was, but the tales written about him and his brave band of knights are very famous.
One story is about the magic sword, Excalibur. The sword lies buried deep in a stone. The only person who can pull it out is the rightful king of Britain. Arthur comes across the stone just at the moment when he needs a sword. Everyone is amazed when he pulls it out easily. Arthur becomes a great king and rules very wisely.

You could make a smaller version of this sword to use as a dagger.

Ready for Battle

Knights often wore chainmail to go into battle. Over the top, a knight wore a tunic with his coat of arms on it. You can wear this fantastic chainmail shirt and tunic with your helmet, shield and sword to complete your knight's outfit.

1 Lay one of the T-shirts on a flat surface.

To make chainmail and tunic you will need

For the chainmail
- 2 grey, long-sleeved T-shirts
- piece of card
- black fabric paint
- tray
- bottle top
- velcro
- glue
- scissors

For the tunic
- fleece fabric 40cm x 120cm
- felt
- glue
- dressing gown cord

2 Pour some black paint into the tray and spread it out using the piece of card. Dip the bottle top in the paint and print circles on to the sleeves of the T-shirt. Overlap the prints to make them look like chainmail. Keep doing this until you have covered the front of the T-shirt and the front of the sleeves. Leave to dry.

3 Turn the T-shirt over and repeat step 2, but this time on the back of the T-shirt.

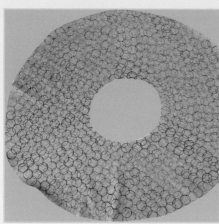
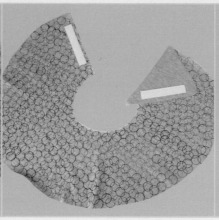

4 For the chainmail collar cut a circle out of the second T-shirt. Cut a small hole in the centre. Follow step 2 to print on the chainmail pattern. Leave to dry.

5 Cut the circle open. Stick a piece of velcro to the two sides as shown.

6 To make the tunic, fold the length of fleece fabric in half. Cut a scoop from the folded edge so that it will fit over your head.

7 Cut out a shield shape from the felt. Copy the template on page 32 for a lion. Glue it on to the front of the tunic.

8 Put on the chainmail T-shirt. Wear the tunic over the top, belted with the dressing gown cord. Put the collar round your neck and fasten it together. With your sword (pages 12 – 13), shield (pages 8 – 9) and helmet (pages 10 – 11), you are now ready to go into battle!

Chivalry

Knights followed a set of rules called the 'code of chivalry'. Before a squire could become a knight he had to promise to be honest, brave and loyal, to protect people weaker than himself, and to fight for the good of everyone – not just for himself.

Knight's Castle Card

A knight's castle often had a water-filled moat around it to keep out attackers. A drawbridge was raised and lowered across the moat to let people in and out. This card has a drawbridge surprise. Lower it to see who is living in the castle.

For a knight's castle card you will need

- thin card 30cm x 15cm
- coloured paper
- wrapping paper
- felt-tip pen
- scissors
- glue
- a small photograph of you or your family
- hole punch
- sharp pencil
- thin ribbon
- glitter

1 Fold the card in half. Use the templates on page 31 to cut three towers from the coloured paper, and five window shapes and a gatehouse from the wrapping paper. Glue the shapes on to the front of the card.

2 Glue the photograph in the middle of the gatehouse 1cm from the bottom. Draw window panes onto the window shapes.

3 To make the drawbridge, cut a rectangle of card the same size as your photograph plus 1cm all the way round. Shape it so that the top is slightly narrower than the bottom. Bend back 1cm of the card at the bottom to make a flap.

4 Punch a hole in each of the top two corners of the drawbridge. Put some glue on the coloured side of the flap and stick it down just under the photograph. When folded up, the drawbridge should cover the photograph.

5 Close your drawbridge and use the holes you have made in the drawbridge as a guide to make holes in the gatehouse with a sharp pencil.

6 Cut two lengths of ribbon and tie a knot in the end of each one. Start at the front of the card with the drawbridge up. Thread one piece of ribbon through one of the drawbridge holes, then through the hole in the gatehouse. Do the same on the other side of the drawbridge.

7 Allow enough ribbon for the drawbridge to open fully. Then tie a knot inside the card and cut off any extra ribbon.

Lower the drawbridge to see who is living in the castle.

8 You can decorate your castle with glitter. Write a message inside your card and pull up the drawbridge.

Crazy Catapult

Castle walls were so thick and strong that it was almost impossible to break them down. Instead armies did a lot of damage by catapulting missiles over the walls. This fun catapult fires silver foil boulders.

To make a crazy catapult you will need

- cardboard tube from the inside of a kitchen roll
- wrapping paper
- 30cm ruler
- silver duct tape
- 8cm rubber band
- matchbox tray
- paint and paintbrush
- double-sided tape
- kitchen foil
- cotton wool balls
- sticky tape

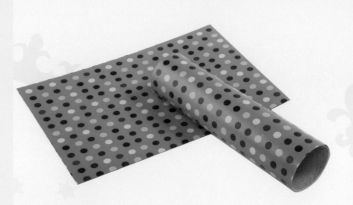

1 Glue wrapping paper on to the tube. Cover the ruler with duct tape.

2 Loop the two ends of the rubber band round the tube.

3 Pass one end of the rubber band through the other. Hold the loop with your finger.

4 Push the ruler through the loop that you are holding. The rubber band should be a quarter of the way along the ruler.

5 Paint the matchbox tray. Leave to dry.

6 Use double-sided tape to fix the painted box to the end of the ruler furthest away from the tube.

7 Make some ammunition to launch from your catapult by scrunching kitchen foil around cotton wool balls to make boulders.

8 Tape the ends of the tube to a work surface. Load a boulder into the box.

9 Take aim and FIRE! Press down quickly on the end of the ruler that is opposite to the box.

Trebuchet

In the Middle Ages one way of attacking a castle was to use a machine called a trebuchet. This was a clever type of catapult that used weights at one end of a long arm to sling heavy boulders high in the air from the other end. Armies used these machines to send showers of rocks and burning straw bales over castle walls until the people inside surrendered.

Jester's Hat Prints

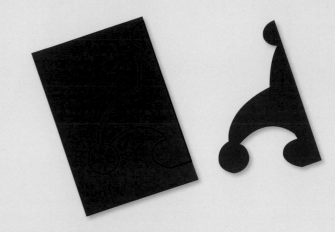

I n medieval times, the court of a wealthy knight would often have a jester to provide entertainment. It was the job of the court jester to be silly and funny and to make everyone laugh. The jester wore a three-pointed hat with bells attached. You can make a jester's hat picture and tell some jokes to make everyone smile.

To make a jester's hat design you will need

- felt-tip pen
- sheets of craft foam
- scissors
- 2 small boxes
- glue
- brightly coloured paint
- baking trays
- small pieces of card
- sheet of paper
- pom-poms

1 Using the template on page 31, draw half of a jester's hat on the foam. Cut it out. Use this cutout as a template to draw round and make a second identical shape.

2 Stick the two foam templates on to the sides of the boxes to make the hat shape (as shown here).

3 Squeeze a blob of paint on to the tray.

4 Spread the blob of paint into a thin layer with a piece of card.

5 Dab one half of the jester's hat on to the paint.

6 Print on to the paper several times. Leave to dry.

7 Repeat step 4 with another colour paint and the second half of the hat. Do not worry about joining the halves up too neatly.

8 Stick the pom-poms to the ends of the points on the hat.

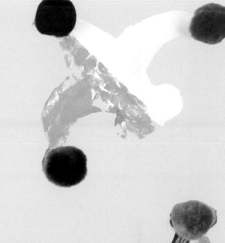

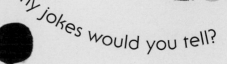

If you were a court jester what funny jokes would you tell?

What do you call a knight who is afraid to fight?

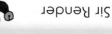

Sir Render

21

Roary the Dragon

According to legend, apart of a knight's job was to kill fierce dragons if they attacked people. But this cute sock dragon is far too friendly to attack anyone! You could hang him up in your bedroom to breathe fire on any bad dreams.

To make this cute dragon you will need

- long sock
- cushion stuffing or clean tights cut into pieces
- felt of different colours
- scissors
- fabric glue
- pins
- 2 polystyrene balls
- blue felt-tip pen
- sheet of craft foam
- needle and thread

1 Fill the sock with the stuffing or shredded tights. You will need to put enough in so that the sock holds its shape.

2 Tie a knot in the open end of the sock.

3 Cut out flame shapes from red, orange and yellow felt. Glue them together. Glue the flames to the toe of the sock, pushing them in a little way to form a mouth.

4 Cut out two pieces of black felt for nostrils. Glue them on either side of the sock above the mouth.

5 Copy the shape on page 30 to cut out two ears from orange felt. Put a blob of glue in the middle of the straight edge of the shape and pinch it together.

6 Attach the ears with a blob of glue on each side of the heel of the sock. Pin in place until the glue has dried. Remove the pins.

7 Using the blue felt-tip pen, colour a blue spot on each of the polystyrene balls.

8 Cut two eyelash shapes from the felt. Glue the eyelashes to the sock on either side of the head, just in front of the ears. Glue a polystyrene ball under each of the lashes.

9 Cut out a pair of foam wings. Glue them to the dragon's back.

10 Ask an adult to push a threaded needle through the dragon near the wings. Knot the end under the head and use the loose end to hang your dragon up.

Your dragon can now fly around, breathing fire as he goes.

George and the Dragon

According to legend, Saint George saved a town – and a beautiful princess – from being terrorised by a fierce dragon. George killed the dragon and rescued the princess. Saint George is the Patron Saint of England.

23

Jousting

Jousting was a sport for knights. It was a test of nerve and skill between two knights on horseback. Both knights carried long poles, called lances. They charged at each other, and the winner was the knight who knocked his opponent off his horse. The knights and their horses wore armour for protection. They also wore colourful tunics made from cloth.

To make a jousting picture you will need

- tracing paper
- soft pencil
- sheet of paper
- sticky tape
- ballpoint pen
- crayons or paints
- glitter glue

1 Trace the shapes on pages 30 – 31 on to the tracing paper.

2 Turn the tracing paper over. Using the soft pencil, scribble over the lines covering them completely.

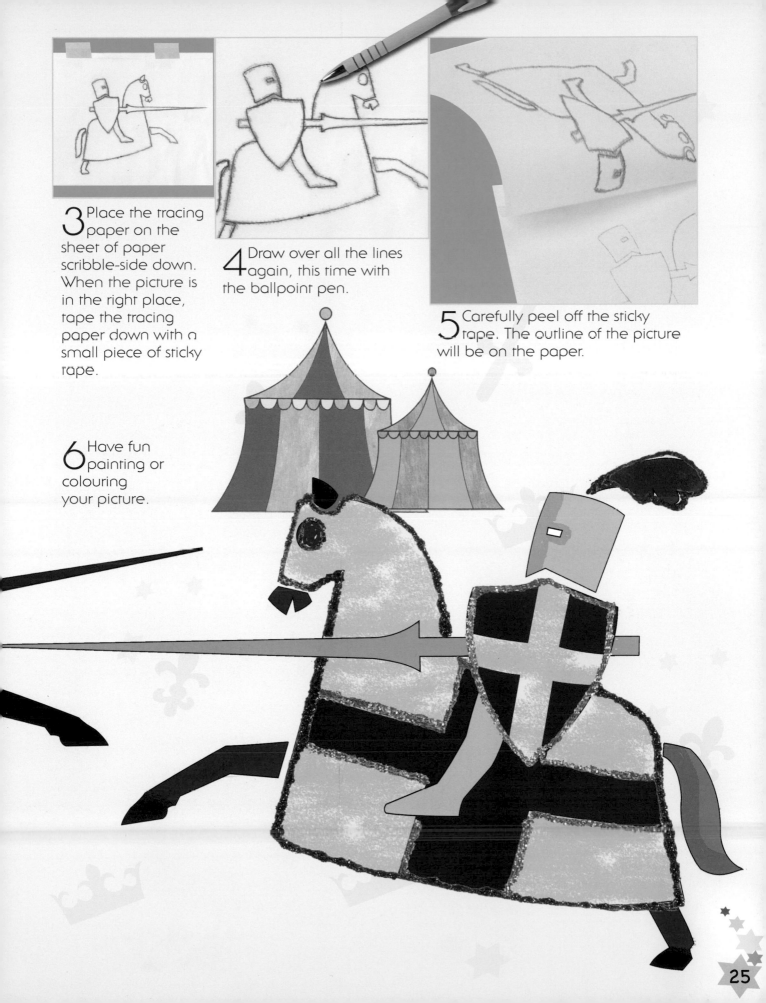

3 Place the tracing paper on the sheet of paper scribble-side down. When the picture is in the right place, tape the tracing paper down with a small piece of sticky tape.

4 Draw over all the lines again, this time with the ballpoint pen.

5 Carefully peel off the sticky tape. The outline of the picture will be on the paper.

6 Have fun painting or colouring your picture.

Drawstring Purses

Medieval knights and their ladies kept coins in drawstring purses made of leather or velvet. They often tied these purses to their belts for safe keeping. These snazzy drawstring purses are decorated with coloured tassels.

To make a drawstring purse you will need

- plate 25cm across the widest part
- fleece or T-shirt fabric – (ask permission before you cut up an old fleece or T-shirt)
- felt-tip pen
- scissors
- hole punch
- thin ribbon or cord
- glitter glue, scraps of felt or fabric

To make a tassel you will need

- thin wool or embroidery thread
- piece of stiff card the length you want the tassel to be
- scissors

Drawstring Purse

1 Place the plate on top of your fabric and draw round it.

2 Use the hole punch to make holes around the edge of the fabric, evenly spaced about 2cm apart.

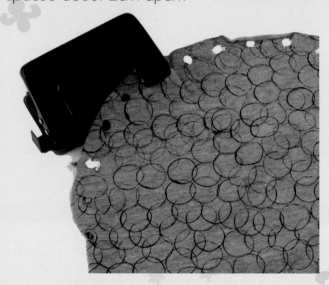

3 Thread the ribbon or cord into one hole and out of the next all the way round the circle. Pull the ribbon or cord to gather up the top of the bag.

Tassel

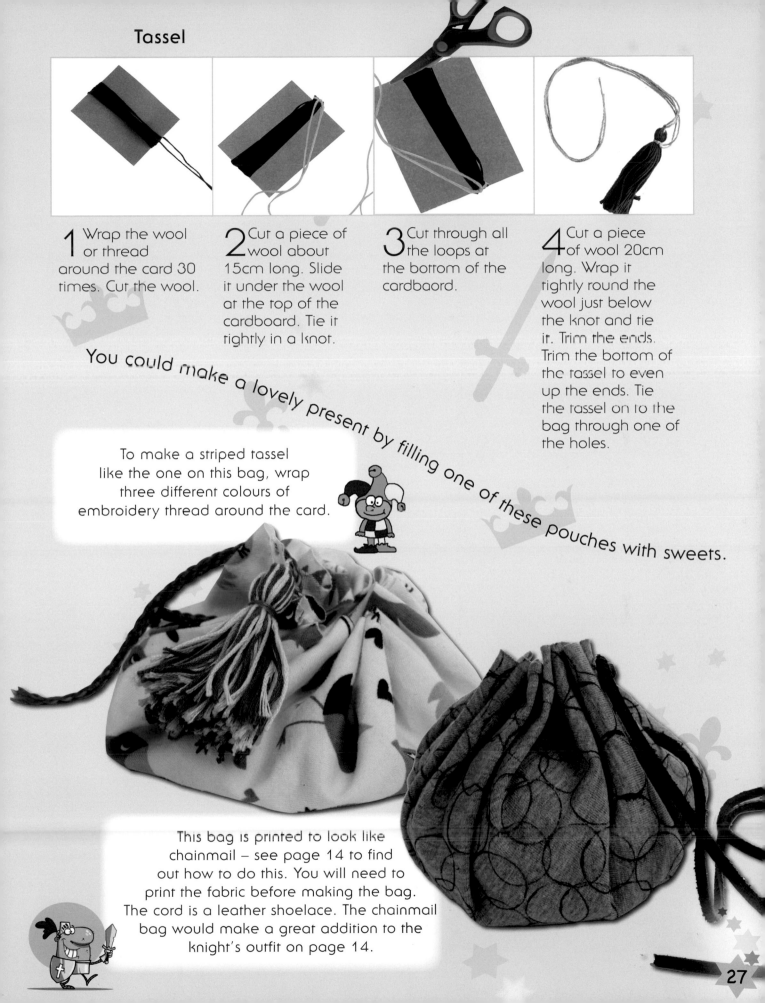

1 Wrap the wool or thread around the card 30 times. Cut the wool.

2 Cut a piece of wool about 15cm long. Slide it under the wool at the top of the cardboard. Tie it tightly in a knot.

3 Cut through all the loops at the bottom of the cardbaord.

4 Cut a piece of wool 20cm long. Wrap it tightly round the wool just below the knot and tie it. Trim the ends. Trim the bottom of the tassel to even up the ends. Tie the tassel on to the bag through one of the holes.

You could make a lovely present by filling one of these pouches with sweets.

To make a striped tassel like the one on this bag, wrap three different colours of embroidery thread around the card.

This bag is printed to look like chainmail – see page 14 to find out how to do this. You will need to print the fabric before making the bag. The cord is a leather shoelace. The chainmail bag would make a great addition to the knight's outfit on page 14.

Castle Picture

In some old churches or castles you might find engraved brass portraits of medieval knights. In recent times, it became a popular hobby to make copies of these pictures by laying sheets of paper on top and gently rubbing across the paper with pencil or wax. You can make your own rubbing pictures using everyday objects from around the house.

For this rubbing picture you will need

- materials with different textures – for example, string, coins, leaves, stickers, safety pins, paperclips, lentils, spaghetti
- scraps of paper
- wax crayons
- card
- glue
- sheet of thin paper

1 To make a rubbing, place a sheet of paper on top of your chosen object and gently rub the wax crayon across the paper. Try a few rubbings on scraps of paper to see what objects work best.

2 Corrugated card has a stripy texture.

3 Paperclips and safety pins make interesting shapes and patterns. You can create great textures with lentil or rice rubbings.

4 Pieces of spaghetti are good for making straight outlines.

5 Leaf rubbings make great pictures. In a scene they look like miniature trees.

6 String can be used to make curved outlines and curly shapes, like this sun. The texture in the centre is made by rubbing over a small coin.

7 A rubbing made from overlapping stickers looks like bricks or stones.

8 When you have collected all the elements you need for your picture stick them on to a piece of card. Place a sheet of paper on top and gently rub different coloured wax crayons over the objects to reveal your magic picture.

Templates

Roary the Dragon
Pages 22 – 23

ear

Defend Yourself
Pages 8 – 9

Jousting
Pages 24 – 25

Knight's Helmet
Pages 10 – 11

30

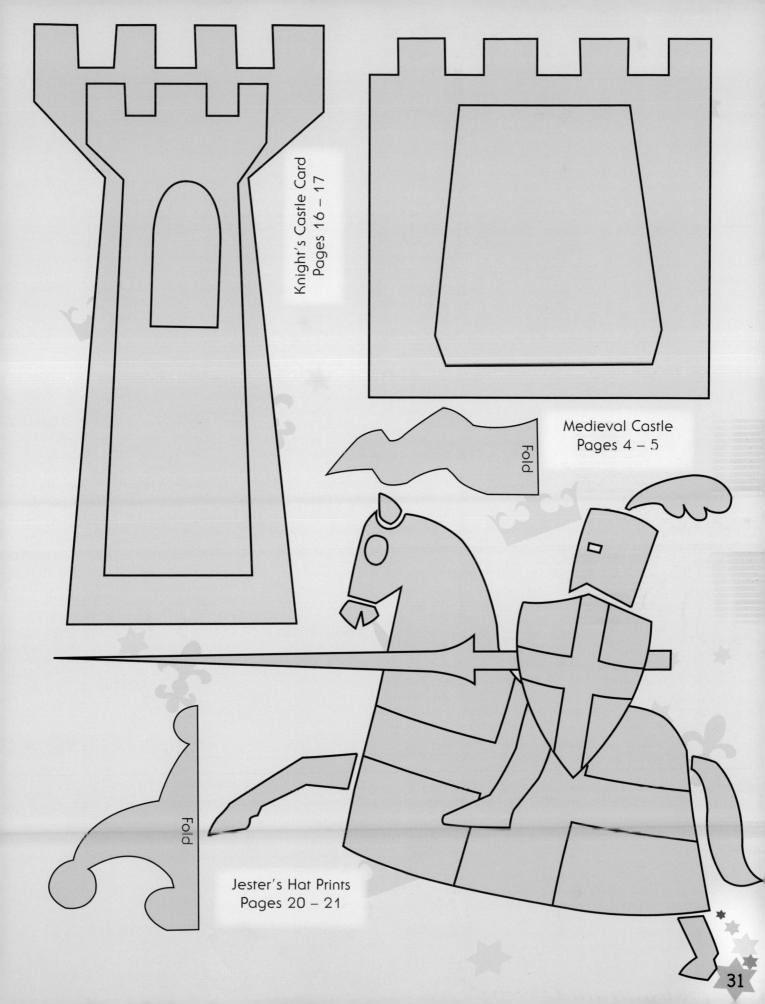

Knight's Castle Card
Pages 16 – 17

Medieval Castle
Pages 4 – 5

Fold

Fold

Jester's Hat Prints
Pages 20 – 21

31

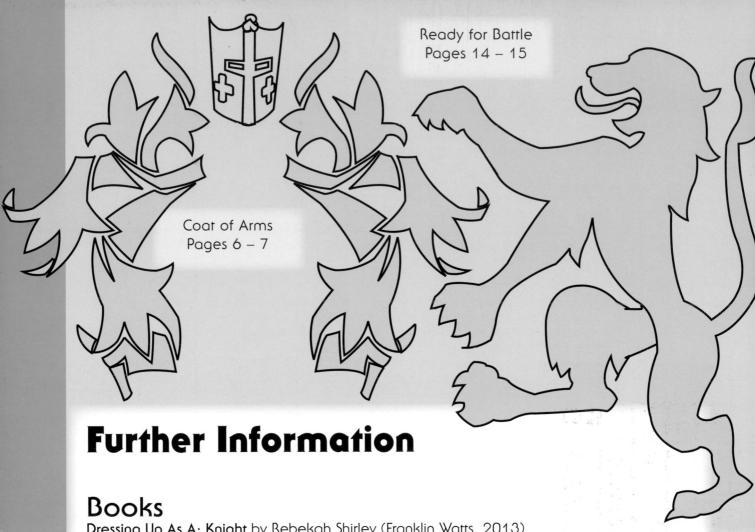

Ready for Battle
Pages 14 – 15

Coat of Arms
Pages 6 – 7

Further Information

Books

Dressing Up As A: Knight by Rebekah Shirley (Franklin Watts, 2013)
Knights and Castles series by Laura Durman and Paul Humphrey (Franklin Watts 2013)
Know It All: Knights by James Nixon (Franklin Watts 2013)

Websites

http://www.vam.ac.uk/vastatic/microsites/british_galleries/designa/coat_of_arms/coat_of_arms.swf
http://www.kathimitchell.com/middleages.htm

Index

armour 6, 24
castle card 16–17
castle picture 28–29
castles 4–5, 9, 16, 17, 18, 19, 28, 29
catapults 18–19
chainmail 14–15, 27

chivalry 15
coat of arms 6–7, 9, 14
dragons 22–23
helmets 6, 7, 10–11, 14, 15
jesters 20–21
jousting 9, 24–25
jousting picture 24–25
King Arthur 13
pages 9

printing 20, 21
purses 26–27
Saint George 23
shields 6, 8–9, 11, 14, 15
squires 9, 11, 15
swords 8, 9, 10, 11, 12–13, 14, 15
trebuchet 19
tunics 6, 14–15, 24